The Cat of Strawberry Hill

A True Story

By Fran Hodgkins • Illustrated by Lesia Sochor

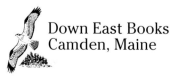

Down East Books
Camden, Maine

Dust-jacket and interior design by Lindy Gifford

Printed in China by Oceanic Graphic Printing Productions Ltd.

5   4   3   2   1

ISBN 0-89272-684-9

Library of Congress Control Number: 2005928858

Down East Books
Camden, Maine
a division of Down East Enterprise, publisher of *Down East* magazine

For catalog information and book orders, call 1-800-685-7962, or visit
www.downeastbooks.com

Thanks to the people of Strawberry Hill Seaside Inn for their help in making this book possible: Dana Burton, Ken Thompson Jr., Cheryl Hocking, Betty Miller, Tammy Rodriques, Shelia Gibbs Fish, and, especially, Violet Burton.

—F.H.

To my dear friend Ethel Pochocki for her wise words and encouragement.

—L.S.

If you stop at the Strawberry Hill Seaside Inn in Rockport, Maine, you'll be greeted by a very important person.

Or, rather, purr-son.

She has eyes that are the color of the sea. Her fur is the brown of the earth in the potato fields of Aroostook County and the white of the snow on Mount Katahdin.

People call her Pumpkin, but she probably had another name long ago. She keeps her secrets and doesn't tell anyone the true story of how she happened to become an inn cat. We know only part of it—that she was found at a rest stop on coastal Route 1 at the end of an October some years ago.

The kitten and her people had driven north to see the autumn leaves. She liked the movement of the car. She purred as she lay in the little girl's lap.

The family stopped for a picnic. The roadside rest stop was all theirs, so they let the kitten out. She scampered among the leaves that swirled in the sea breeze and made irresistible rustles.

While the kitten played and her family ate, another car pulled into the rest stop. The kitten hardly noticed; she was too busy stalking a maple leaf.

The big black dog in the newly arrived car noticed her, though. He charged out, barking, and ran straight for the sea-eyed kitten.

The kitten ran. She could hear only the dog, feel his hot breath on her back. Suddenly, she tumbled off the edge of a cliff. Down, down, down she rolled. She heard voices calling for her, and she heard the big dog barking.

Then everything went dark.

An hour later, with a sharp pain in her hind paw, the kitten jerked awake. A big gray and white herring gull had nipped at her. He rose into the air, squawking with surprise.

The kitten shook her paw and licked her tail. She climbed back up over the rocks, back toward her people.

But both cars were gone.

Frightened and alone, the kitten curled up under the picnic table. She could still smell her people: The man with his beard that she liked to touch. The woman who hummed as she brushed the kitten's fur. The little girl who was warm to sleep next to. In time, the kitten fell asleep, and dreams took the place of memories.

The crunch of tires on gravel woke her. Another car? Another dog? The sea-eyed kitten trembled and made herself as small as she could.

There was no dog. Just two people, a man and a woman. No little girl. These were not her people.

The man and woman stood looking out at the sea. They smelled of coffee, and the kitten knew that coffee meant breakfast and that breakfast meant food. She mewed. They didn't hear her.

The man looked at his watch. "We should go," he said.

The kitten mewed again, louder this time, and ventured out from under the table.

"Look!" said the woman. "Isn't she pretty?" Now the kitten could smell other cats as well as coffee. She hurried over and let the woman pick her up.

"Where do you think she belongs?" the man asked.

"She must be frightened," the woman said. "It's a shame to think someone lost such a little one."

"Do you think . . . ?" the man began.

The woman shook her head. "Two cats at home is plenty." Then she smiled. "But she could stay at the inn."

So the sea-eyed kitten went to live at the Strawberry Hill Seaside Inn, which was owned and run by the people who had found her. At first she was wary of the big pumpkins that decorated the lobby, but soon she found them good to sit on to watch the guests who came and went. In fact, she spent so much time among the pumpkins that the woman decided the kitten should share their name!

Many of the guests stroked her soft fur, and their children were always happy to see her. She would walk with them down the path as they admired the trees and ocean.

Fewer people came during the winter. But there were still jobs for Pumpkin to do. She supervised the making of the fire in the woodstove. And stayed nearby to make sure it didn't go out.

She helped the innkeepers gather the laundry. Then she sat in the laundry room to watch the linens and towels spin in the big washing machine. She liked the bubbles and the *swoosh* of the water.

She leapt to the windowsill and made little sounds in her throat as she stared for hours at the little black-capped chickadees that dashed to and from the big bird feeder just outside.

Spring brought more people, and summer still more. Just as she had in the fall and the winter, Pumpkin greeted the guests with a wave of her banner tail. She followed them to their rooms as they unloaded their bags. She watched as children and parents splashed in the swimming pool. She yawned as early risers came to the lobby for coffee and as late-night arrivals checked in after dark. When guests snoozed outside in the wooden Adirondack chairs overlooking Penobscot Bay, she would take time from her day and sit quietly with them.

Now, years have passed since that frightening day when she lost her people. But Pumpkin has found another family, one that grows with the arrival of every new inn guest.

If you visit the inn and sit very quietly in one of the Adirondack chairs, she might come to you, rub around your ankles, and then settle into your lap.

Her purrs will tell you stories of the sea and the sky. But she will never tell you where she came from.

She is the cat of Strawberry Hill.

Author's Note

Every year, vacationers lose thousands of pets as they travel, whether by accident or design. Lucky animals, like Pumpkin, are found by caring people who adopt them or bring them to animal shelters. A portion of the proceeds from this book will go to support the animal shelters of Camden, Rockport, and Rockland, Maine.